The Canon Of Holy Scripture: With Remarks Upon King James's Version , The Latin Vulgate And Douay Bible

Matthew Henry Henderson

FRANCIS & LOUTREL,
PRINTERS,
NEW YORK.

Is the English Bible the Word of God?

---•••---

The Canon of Holy Scripture.

THE

Canon of Holy Scripture:

WITH REMARKS UPON

KING JAMES'S VERSION, THE LATIN VULGATE AND DOUAY BIBLE.

BY

MATTHEW H. HENDERSON, D. D.,

RECTOR OF EMMANUEL CHURCH, ATHENS, GEORGIA,
FORMERLY RECTOR OF TRINITY CHURCH,
NEWARK, N. J.

———•••———

New York:
POTT & AMERY,
Nos. 5 & 13 Cooper Union.
1868.

PREFACE.

———————

THE brief treatise on the CANON OF HOLY SCRIPTURE, now presented to the reader, was published in 1853, when the author was Rector of Trinity Church, Newark, N. J. It having fallen out of print entirely, and the author having often been inquired of for copies of it, he determined to revise it carefully, and then re-issue it in a more compact form, and in such shape as to render it adapted for use as a convenient and reliable manual. He is the more readily persuaded to this course, because the subject is one that can never grow old, and one which assumes the gravest importance as Romanism increases in strength in our country, and as it is its purpose, whenever and wherever possible, to crush out of existence the pure word of God which is contained in the English Bible.

M. H. H.

ATHENS, GA.,
September 10th, 1868.

BOOK OF COMMMON PRAYER.

BLESSED LORD, who hast caused all Holy Scriptures to be written for our learning; grant that we may in such wise hear them, read, mark, learn, and inwardly digest them. that by patience, and comfort of thy holy Word, we may embrace and ever hold fast the blessed hope of everlasting life, which thou hast given us in our Saviour Jesus Christ. Amen.— *Collect for the Second Sunday in Advent.*

HOLY SCRIPTURE.

"ALL *Scripture.* inspired of God, is profitable to teach, to reprove, to correct, to instruct in justice, that the man of God may be perfect, furnished to every good work."—*Douay Bible*, 2 Tim. iii. 16.

"Search the Scriptures."—*Douay Bible*, John v. 29.

"I had rather speak five words with my understanding, that I may instruct others also; than ten thousand words in a tongue."—*Douay Bible*, 1 Cor. xiv. 19.

ROMISH COUNCIL.

"*That the Laity may not have the Books of Scripture, except the Psalter and the divine office, and not even these Books in the vulgar tongue.*"

"We also prohibit the laity to have the Books of the Old Testament or of the New, unless, perhaps, that some might desire, for devotion, to have the *Psalter* or the *Breviary* for the divine offices, or the hours of the blessed Mary. BUT WE MOST STRICTLY FORBID THEM TO HAVE THESE BOOKS TRANSLATED INTO THE VULGAR TONGUE."—Toulouse, A. D. 1229. (Under St. Angelus, Cardinal and Legate of the Pope.) See Appendix for the original.

HISTORY.

"Within the last five years sixty thousand Roman Catholics . . . have dissolved their connection with the Roman Catholic Church, avowed their Protestantism, and joined, the most of them, the Church of England." "The Irish Scriptures, *put into the hands of the people,* are confessedly at the bottom of these conversions." "Previous to A. D. 1846, some hundreds of thousands of the native Irish had been taught to *read the Scriptures in their own language.*"—Bishop De Lancey, *Address to the Convention, in* 1852.

THE

Canon of Holy Scripture.

———•◦•———

HEBREWS i. 1, 2.

"GOD, WHO AT SUNDRY TIMES AND IN DIVERS MANNERS SPAKE IN TIME PAST UNTO THE FATHERS BY THE PROPHETS, HATH IN THESE LAST DAYS SPOKEN UNTO US BY HIS SON."

THAT God should make himself known to man, the Creator to his intelligent and immortal creature, is a thing which right reason deems neither impossible nor improbable. In no other way can we arrive at any just conception or sure knowledge of his Divine will.

God's image and superscription, indeed, are written upon his works. They tell of his being and power and intelligence. But they do not and cannot declare to us his whole will and character. While the things around us indicate design,* and their tendencies indicate benevolence on the part of the

* Paley's "*Moral Philosophy*," Book II., ch. v.

Designer, still there is so much of perplexity in their actual working; there are so many cross rays breaking and discoloring the main stream of light, that our conjectures and persuasions never can amount to certain convictions. We need, therefore, some direct communication to assure us of the real character of God. We require that our dim surmises should be authorized by authentic declarations of his will. Natural religion affords us the hypothesis. Revelation only can supply the proof. "If any man think," says Lord Bacon, "by view and inquiry into sensible and material things to attain to any light for the revealing of the nature or the will of God, he shall dangerously abuse himself. It is true that the contemplation of the creatures of God hath for end, as to the nature of the *creatures themselves, knowledge :* but as to the *nature of God,* no knowledge, but *wonder ;* which is nothing else but contemplation broken off or losing itself. . . . Therefore attend his *will* as *himself* openeth it, and give unto faith that which unto faith belongeth, for more worthy it is to believe than to think or know."

While, therefore, his power and Godhead are manifested by the things which he hath made, there must be something else to disclose his mind and will. And this disclosure *hath been made,* even *in* and *by Him,* who is "'the brightness of his Father's glory, and the express image of his person;' who came forth from the inscrutable recesses of Deity; the

outward representative of the inward mind; 'God
of God; Light of Light; very God of very God :'*
the Son of the Father; the Word,—the intelligible
declaration of the otherwise unintelligible will. 'No
man hath seen God at any time; the only-begotten
Son which is in the bosom of the Father, he hath
declared him;' acted as his interpreter; come forth
from the inaccessible throne of the mysterious Godhead, the Priest and Mediator of his will. That
which is not Himself, that which is created only—
mute, material nature—may proclaim his power;
but Himself alone, that which is generated from him,
may proclaim his mind and heart."†

It would seem thus as if every manifestation of
God made to his intelligent creation must come
through the medium of his Son. Even the Prophets
of old were inspired, as St. Peter tells us, by the
Spirit of Christ;‡ and through this they "testified
beforehand" of his "sufferings, and the glory that
should follow."

That God *has* so revealed himself is a fact established by the strongest possible proof. Miracles and
prophecy were the credentials of his messengers.
The supernatural power which they wielded, and
the supernatural knowledge which they possessed,
showed that they were commissioned from on high.
From Moses, down to our Lord Jesus Christ himself

* Nicene Creed.   † Griffith's "*Sermons.*"
‡ 1 St. Peter i. 11.

and the last of his Apostles, these were the seals of the Divine commission;—the token and proof that they were in very deed the ministers and messengers of God. So it was the Apostle wrote, in words of truth and soberness: "God, who at sundry times and in divers manners spake in time past unto the fathers by the Prophets, hath in these last days spoken unto us by *His Son*, whom he hath appointed heir of all things, by whom also he made the worlds; who, being the brightness of his glory, and the express image of his person, and upholding all things by the word of his power, when he had by himself purged our sins, sat down upon the right hand of the Majesty on high." With solemn emphasis and pregnant meaning does he exhort immediately afterwards: "Therefore we ought to give the more earnest heed to the things which we have heard, lest at any time we should let them slip. For if the word spoken by angels was steadfast, and every transgression and disobedience received a just recompense of reward; how shall we escape, if we neglect so great salvation; which at the first began to be spoken by the Lord, and was confirmed unto us by them that heard him, *God also bearing them witness, both with signs and wonders, and with divers miracles and gifts of the Holy Ghost.*"*

Now this *revelation* of his will and character which God's mercy hath made, his wisdom has *caused to*

* Heb. ii. 1-4.

be written, that thus it might be preserved for all time, the sure guide and stay of man in all his wanderings and weakness. "For whatsoever things were written aforetime, were written for our learning; that we, through patience and comfort of the Scriptures, might have hope."* With his own finger He traced upon the rocky tablet the everlasting law, and raised up men from time to time,—the Prophets of old,—whom He inspired in the utterance and guided in the record of his truth. Thus "Moses *wrote* all the words of the LORD."† Thus Jeremiah was instructed to make record of the Divine revelation : "*Write* all the words that I have spoken unto thee *in a book.*"‡ Thus St. Luke, as he himself declares, set forth and "*wrote in order*" his Gospel; "a declaration of those things which are most surely believed;" that believers "*might know the certainty* of those things wherein they had been instructed."§

I need not stop to show the wisdom of the arrangement which has thus placed the revelation of God to man in the indelible characters of a written language. "*Litera scripta manet.*" There are permanence and certainty in the authentic record, which can be predicated of nothing else. We want, indeed, no stronger illustration of the utter worthlessness of mere oral tradition, as contrasted with

---

* Rom. xv. 4. † Exod. xxiv. 4.
‡ Jer. xxx. 2. § St. Luke i. 1.

the written word, for the transmission of truth, than the fact to which our Saviour refers, in his pointed rebuke of the Scribes and Pharisees;—"Ye have made the commandment of God of none effect by your tradition."*

That the Inspired Writers should make use of their vernacular tongue, or a language generally used and understood at the time, for the record of the Divine truth which had been communicated to them, was a thing naturally to be expected. Hence the books of the *Old Testament* Scriptures, with but few exceptions, were written in *Hebrew.* Small portions of Daniel and Ezra, and a few words in Jeremiah, were written in the Chaldaic,† with which language the Jews became acquainted at the Babylonish captivity. After this period the Hebrew seems to have fallen gradually into disuse, except among the Priests and Levites, and the educated classes of the Jewish people. The Hebrew language has been thought by some critics to have been that which was spoken in Paradise ; but, while this can hardly be affirmed with any probability, it is certainly true that it is one of the most ancient languages in the world. Traces of the Hebrew are found in the Chaldee, Syriac, Arabic, Persian, Phœnician, and the languages of other neighboring

* St. Matt. xv. 6.

† Jer. x. 11, Dan. ii. 4, to the end of chap. vii., and Ezra iv. 8. to vi. 19. and vii. 12 to 27, are written in the Chaldee dialect.

countries; a fact which has been adduced in favor of its great antiquity.*

The *New Testament* Scriptures were written in *Greek*, by the authors to whom the several books are attributed; because, although the Syro-Chaldaic was their vernacular tongue, yet the Greek was used and well understood throughout the greater part of the known world, especially in the Eastern provinces of the Roman Empire.

The precious manuscripts of the Old Testament in Hebrew were preserved by the Jews with the most scrupulous fidelity. Copies were made with the utmost possible care, and the least variation in the most minute particular was counted sufficient to condemn them.† The Old Testament was

---

* The letters of the alphabet, amounting to twenty-two, were written originally in the form of the old character, which is called the Samaritan. The square form in which we now find them was taken from the Chaldæans about the time of the Babylonish captivity, as some think; or, as others maintain, about the commencement of the Christian era.

† After the return of the Jews from the Babylonish captivity (B. C. 535), the books of the Law and the Prophets were publicly read in their synagogues every Sabbath day; which was an excellent method of securing their purity, as well as of enforcing the observation of the law. The Chaldee paraphrases, and the translation of the Old Testament into Greek, which were afterwards made, were so many additional securities. To these facts we may add, that the reverence of the Jews for their sacred writings is another guarantee for their integrity; so great indeed was that reverence, that, according to the statements of Philo and Josephus, they would suffer any torments, and even death itself, rather than change a single point or iota of the Scriptures. A law was also enacted by them, which denounced him to be guilty of inexpiable

translated into *Greek* at Alexandria, probably about
B. C. 285 or 286, for the use of the devout Jews
who dwelt in large numbers at that time in Egypt,
and who used that language in their ordinary
intercourse. It is supposed to have derived its
name (*the Septuagint*) from the number* of persons
employed in its translation. Translations were
made from this (the Septuagint), certainly into
Latin, in the second century; and soon after into
Ethiopic or Abyssinian, and Egyptian, *i. e.*, Coptic
and Sahidic. There was also a translation made
into Syriac, directly from the Hebrew, about the
beginning of the same (second) century. All these
have been providentially preserved.

It is easy to see how these several versions would
be faithful conservators of the truth; each being a
guard and check upon the others, to prevent any
change or variation from ignorance, accident, or
design. Beside the watchful care of the Jews, before the time of our Saviour, to preserve the Sacred
Writings intact and uncorrupt; and the jealousy
between them and the Christians subsequent to
that time, which would immediately have detected
and published any accidental or designed variation
from the original; this single fact is abundant

sin who should presume to make the slightest possible alteration in
their sacred books.—Horne's "*Introduction*," Vol. I, Ch. ii. Sec. 3,
p. 113.

* *Septuaginta* means seventy. See the very elaborate article on the
SEPTUAGINT, by Dr. Selwyn, in Smith's "*Dictionary of the Bible.*"

proof of the undoubted preservation of the original text; viz., the agreement of all the manuscripts of the Old Testament, amounting to about eleven hundred, which are known to be extant. These manuscripts* are, indeed, of different dates, and are not all entire—some containing but comparatively small portions of the Sacred Volume; but apart from errors and mistakes, resulting from the carelessness or inaccuracy of copyists, and occasional variations where they help to correct each other, they harmonize so well as not to throw doubt on any important passage, and to confirm the received text in every essential particular.

The following circumstance will show the wonderful harmony of the different manuscripts of the Old Testament. Dr. Buchanan, not very many years since (A. D. 1806), brought from India a roll of the Pentateuch, now in the Library at Cambridge, England, which he procured from the Black Jews in Malabar, who are believed to be a remnant of the first dispersion of that nation by Nebuchadnezzar. The date of this manuscript, which is written upon goat-skins dyed red, cannot now be ascertained; but its text is supposed to be derived from those copies which their ancestors brought with them

---

* Few Hebrew manuscripts now extant are supposed to be older than the eleventh or twelfth century. Some Greek manuscripts are very much older, as also one in Gothic. For further remarks as to the number, value, antiquity, etc., of the Greek MSS., see *infra*, pp. 18-20, with the notes.

into India. It measures forty-eight feet in length,* and in breadth about twenty-two inches, or a Jewish cubit. Now a strict investigation has shown that this manuscript, thus brought down through a distinct and independent channel, does not contain more than forty variations from the commonly received Hebrew text;—variations consisting altogether of the addition or omission of unimportant letters which by no means affect the sense.†

Nor should I omit to mention that the Samaritans have preserved the Pentateuch in the old Hebrew character,‡ with unimportant variations, from a period of probably some seven hundred years before the advent of our Lord. This fact, under the circumstances of the case, there having been no friendly intercourse between them and the Jews since the Babylonish captivity, is one among many proofs that the books, which bear his name, were indeed written by the great Jewish lawgiver.

The same observations apply with equal force to the Scriptures of the *New* Testament. The Greek

* The original length must have been not less than ninety feet; as Leviticus and the greater part of Deuteronomy are wanting. Horne, Vol. II., Part I., Ch. ii., Sec. 1; Buchanan's " *Christian Researches*," p. 224, 4th edition.

† Mr. Thomas Yeates's " *Collation of an Indian copy of the Pentateuch*," etc., pp. 2, 3, 6, 7 (1812).

‡ See the " *London Polyglott*," by Bishop Walton (six vols. fol., 1657). Consult also a learned discussion respecting the SAMARITAN PENTATEUCH, in Smith's "*Dictionary of the Bible.*"

originals, the autographs of the Apostles, have, of
course, in the very nature of things, long since
perished. Copies, however, were made and multi-
plied so soon as the Gospels and other books became known to the Churches in different regions,
and *Versions* were made into the different languages
of the nations converted to Christianity, shortly
after St. John, at Patmos, completed the Canon of
Holy Scriptures in the Apocalypse, about A. D. 96.
Thus the old *Syriac* version, or Peshito, *i. e.*, right,
exact, was made, if not in the first century, certainly
in the beginning of the second, and now constitutes
one of the most precious legacies of the early Christian Church. A beautiful and correct edition published in London, 1816, for the Syrian Christians in
India, was received by them with the utmost grati-
tude; the English Church thus repaying her Eastern
sister for her watchful preservation of the sacred
text. Soon afterwards, in the third or fourth century, translations were made into Egyptian, Ethiopic, Armenian, and Gothic. A translation of the
whole Scriptures was made into Latin, early in the
second century, which stood pre-eminent for its
clearness and fidelity amid the numerous versions
which were made at that time, as St. Augustine
testifies, into that language. This was called the
Itala, or *old Italic* version. In consequence, however, of errors and discrepancies, the result of
various causes, a new translation was made by

St. Jerome, about the close of the fourth century, which forms the basis of the present Latin Vulgate of the Roman Catholic Church.*

Various *Manuscripts,* in different languages, of different portions of the New Testament, now in existence, are of very great antiquity.† Some of them are supposed to have been written in the third or fourth century, and are preserved with great care in the public libraries of Europe. In one of these, a Greek manuscript now in the Cottonian Library in the British Museum, is contained a fragment of the Four Gospels, written in letters of silver upon a faded purple ground; the words *Jesus,* and *God,* and *Saviour,* and *Son,* and *Lord,*

---

* St. Jerome began this important work about A. D. 390, and finished it about A. D. 404, when this great biblical scholar was in his seventy-ninth year.

† The Greek manuscripts which have descended to our times were either on vellum or on paper, and prior to the ninth century were written without any separation of words. Very few contain the whole either of the Old or the New Testament. The greater part have only the Four Gospels. In consequence of the scarcity of parchment, whole books were at times obliterated, to make them answer for the works of more recent or favorite authors. Hence, doubtless, many valuable works have perished,—and the more valuable, because the most ancient, were probably the first to perish,—by reason of their having grown dim through age. These manuscripts are called *Codices Rescripti* (re-written). In general they are easily recognized by the traces of the original writing. In a few instances both writings are legible. In one of these, —Codex Ephremi, or Regius, is preserved in great measure the whole Greek Bible. Over the first part of this manuscript has been written (in the twelfth century) some works of Ephrem the Syrian, the original having been partially erased.

being written in letters of gold. This precious fragment is acknowledged to have been executed at the end of the *fourth* or the beginning of the *fifth* century. Another manuscript of the Four Gospels, in the Gothic version, of nearly equal antiquity, now in the University of Upsal, was written in a similar way. There is no work of antiquity handed down in anything like the number of manuscripts that we have of the New Testament. Written in distant and different parts of the world; some of them more than twelve to fourteen hundred years ago, and agreeing with each other in every important particular; they furnish a body of evidence in regard to the uncorrupted preservation of the sacred text which is perfectly conclusive.*

---

* "The manuscripts of the New Testament which are extant are far more numerous than those of any single classic author whomsoever: upwards of three hundred and fifty were collated by *Griesbach*, for his celebrated critical edition. These manuscripts, it is true, are not all entire; most of them contain only the Gospels; others, the Gospels, Acts of the Apostles, and the Epistles; and a few contain the Apocalypse, or Revelation of John. But they were all written in very different and distant parts of the world; several of them are upwards of twelve hundred years old, and give us the books of the New Testament, in all essential points, perfectly accordant with each other, as any person may readily ascertain by examining the critical editions published. The *thirty thousand* various readings which are said to be found in the manuscripts collated by Dr. *Mill*, and the *hundred and fifty thousand* which Griesbach's edition is said to contain, in no degree whatever affect the general credit and integrity of the text. Of this formidable mass of various readings, which have been collected by the diligence of collators, not one-tenth, nay, not one-hundredth part, either *makes* or *can* make any perceptible, or at least any material

When, besides these versions and manuscripts, we take into consideration the frequent and copious quotations which were made from the New Testament Scriptures by the ancient fathers whose works have come down to us—so frequent and copious that, it has been said, the whole Gospel and all the Epistles might be compiled from that source alone,—we may form some idea of the impregnable defences with which God, in his wise Providence, has hedged in the Sacred Record, the Gospel of our salvation. If the shadow of a doubt can be thrown upon the integrity or the authenticity of that Blessed Volume, the charter of our spiritual life and liberty, then all certainty as to the past is at an end; history is a blank; and man's existence a riddle, disjointed and unmeaning as the leaves which the Sibyl scattered to the winds.

The first Saxon version of which we have authentic record, was a translation of the Psalms by Ad-

---

alteration in the sense in any modern version. They consist almost wholly of palpable errors in transcription, grammatical and verbal differences, such as the insertion or omission of an article, the substitution of a word for its equivalent, and the transposition of a word or two in a sentence. Even the few that do change the sense, affect it only in passages relating to unimportant, historical, and geographical circumstances, or other collateral matters; and the still smaller number that make any alteration in things of consequence, do not on that account place us in any absolute uncertainty. . . . The very *worst manuscript extant would not pervert one article of our faith or destroy one moral precept.*"—Horne's "*Introduction to the Critical Study of the Scriptures,*" Vol. I., ch. ii., sec. 3, pp. 117, 118.

helm, Bishop of Sherborne, into that tongue, about A. D. 706.* Some twenty or thirty years after, the Gospel of St. John was translated into Saxon by the Venerable Bede. The *first* English version of the Bible now extant was executed, as is supposed, about A. D. 1290;† the author unknown. *John Wycliffe* rendered the entire Bible from the Latin Vulgate into the English language, as then spoken, about A. D. 1380. The first *printed* English translation of the New Testament was made by Wm. Tyndal, and printed in 1526. In 1535, the *whole* Bible in English was printed by Miles Coverdale, who afterwards was made Bishop of Exeter by Edward VI. Besides these, others were printed,—Matthew's in 1537, Cranmer's and Taverner's in 1539, the Geneva Bible in 1560, and the Bishops' Bible, under the auspices of Archbishop Parker, in 1568. In 1582, the *Romanists,* "finding it," as Horne observes,

---

* For a fuller account of the several English versions, see Horne's "*Introduction,*" Vol. II., Pt. I., ch. vi.; Anthony Johnson's "*Historical Account of the English Translations,*" in Bishop Watson's collection of Theological Tracts; Lewis's "*History of the Translations of the Bible,*" prefixed to Wycliffe's New Testament; and Archbishop Newcome's "*View of the English Biblical Translations.*" (See Appendix at the end.) Smith's "*Dictionary of the Bible,*" under the article Versions, may also be consulted to advantage.

† Bishop Short throws some doubt upon this. He says the oldest English translation now extant is due to a priest of the name of Rolle, who was a hermit at Hampole, in Yorkshire, and translated the Psalms and several other canticles from the Scriptures. He died in 1349.— "*History of the Church of England,*" Appendix D to Chap. xii.

"impossible to withhold the Scriptures from the common people, printed an English New Testament at Rheims." This was translated, not from the original Greek, but from the Latin, being thus a *translation from a translation.* The Old Testament was printed by them at Douay, in 1609, and is therefore called the Douay Bible. This was also translated from the Latin Vulgate.

The authorized translation now in use is commonly called King James's Bible, because revised and printed in his reign. It was undertaken at his command, by reason of objections made to the Bishops' Bible, at the Conference held at Hampton Court, in 1604; and fifty-four learned men,—men pre-eminently distinguished for their knowledge of the original languages in which the Scriptures were written,—were appointed for the important work.* Seven of these, however, either died or declined the task; for the list given by Fuller, in his Church History,† comprises but forty-seven names. After the diligent labor of nearly three years, it was published in folio, in A. D. 1611.

So thoroughly correct was this version found to be, and into such universal esteem did it come soon after its publication, that all others gradually fell into disuse. And now for more than two centuries

---

* See a "*Vindication of the Authorized Translation and Translators of the Bible,*" by Rev. H. J. Todd, M. A. London, 1819.

† Book x., p. 44.

and a half it has held its high place in the judgment of the Christian world, for its general fidelity, perspicuity and excellence. True, it has its faults; but most unquestionably, it approaches as near to perfection as human infirmity will permit. In every fact and doctrine, in spirit and in letter, I believe it to be, from some personal acquaintance with the originals, a full and faithful copy and transcript thereof. Nor is this its only praise. "Our translators have not only made a *standard translation*, but they have made their translation the *standard of our language.* So that after the lapse of two hundred years, the English Bible is, with very few exceptions, the standard of the purity and excellence of the English tongue."* And I have faith to believe will remain so, while the English language is spoken on earth; aye, until all earth's languages are lost and merged in the one universal, eternal language of heaven!† The English Bible "lives on the ear like music that can never be forgotten. It is part of the national mind, and the anchor of national seriousness. The memory of the dead passes into it. The potent traditions of childhood are stereotyped in its verses. The power of all the griefs and trials of a man is hidden beneath its words. It is the representative

---

* Dr. Adam Clarke's *General Preface to his Commentary on the Bible.*

† Multæ terricolis linguæ, cœlestibus una.

of his best moments; and all that there has been about him of soft, and gentle, and pure, and penitent, and good, speaks to him forever out of his English Bible. It is his sacred thing, which doubt has never dimmed and controversy never soiled. In the length and breadth of the land, there is not a Protestant, with one spark of religiousness about him, whose spiritual biography is not in his Saxon Bible."*

This version of the Holy Scriptures, however, has been called "a corrupt and mutilated copy of the Sacred Record of God's most holy will and revelation to man;" while "it purports to be a full and correct copy of the Holy Bible."†

In making some observations on the points involved in this reckless assertion, I desire to speak,

---

* From an article in the *Dublin* (R. Catholic) *Review*, June, 1853, from the pen of a pervert (F. W. Faber).

† Rev. P. Moran, Pastor of St. John's (Roman Catholic) Church, in the *Newark Daily Advertiser*. Mr. Moran bases this charge on the ground that "the Protestant translation does not express the true meaning of the original," and "the suppression of several books and parts of books, contained in the Latin Vulgate, and held as canonical by the Holy Catholic (Romish) Church;" while he affirms that there can be "no logical adjustment" of differences, "because there is no final judge of controversy" to whom mutual submission would be rendered. "We want," he says, "an *infallible* judge, in whose decision we may confidently abide." Archbishop Purcell, of Cincinnati, also calls this version—in an address recently published—"a mutilated and spurious edition of the Scriptures." Of course the Vulgate and Douay Bibles are claimed to be what King James's Bible is not, they having the sanction of an infallible judge.

as with perfect frankness, so with all kindly feeling towards those who differ. It will lead me to speak,

FIRST, Of the *claims* thus put forth in behalf of the LATIN VULGATE and the DOUAY BIBLE; and then, ·

SECOND, of the *true number of* THE CANONICAL BOOKS of the Holy Scriptures.

I. The LATIN VULGATE is unquestionably one of the most valuable legacies of the early Church; being generally a faithful copy of the original Scriptures. It constitutes an efficient help in the arduous labors of the Biblical student. We have, then, no fault to find with the Vulgate in itself; though many errors be admitted, as well as wide departures from the original Hebrew. We find fault with it only as exalted into the place of the original—yea, even above the original itself,—as the absolute, perfect and exact transcript of God's will in every particular, on the ground of *"the decision of an infallible judge."**

* The writer is sometimes asked, " Where the infallibility lies in the Romish Church?" The question is susceptible of a copious, if not satisfactory, answer. It *lies* in *the Pope.* Or if not there, it *lies* in a *General* (*i. e.* Romish) *Council, e. g.* Trent. Or if it be not in either of these, and there are strong Romish authorities for each, it *lies in both combined.* Or if not there, it *lies* in the *Universal* (Roman Catholic) *Church.* The thing has not yet been definitely settled. The inquirer is at liberty to select for himself.—But " how, then, is it rendered available for the guidance of faith?" Manifestly *through the Priest.* To all

This assumption we confidently rebut on the following grounds:—

1. Because the Vulgate version now in existence, and put forth in the sixteenth century, is not that which was made by St. Jerome about A. D. 390. So many errors and discrepancies had crept into the text in the long interval, that much care and renewed revision were necessary to put it in its present form. And there can be no certainty, admitting St. Jerome's version to have been faultless, that this exactly accords with it.

practical intents and purposes, the *Priest* is *the only real infallible guide in the Romish Church;*—the cock and conduit through which flows, as occasion serves or requires, any desirable amount of infallibility, from the great and somewhat indefinitely located and unapproachable reservoir behind. And this is both natural and necessary on the Romish theory. For if God would not leave his Church without an infallible guide, he certainly would not leave it without ready access to that guide; else the very reason of its existence would be gone. Therefore the end of all doubt and controversy is the decision of the Priest. What does the Priest say? The Priest says thus and so. 'For as to the Pope's infallibility, I cannot think that the good and wise God should either have appointed any one man, or any set number of men, as an infallible judge and interpreter of his will, to whom we must attend and obey, resigning up our judgment and reason, and yet never tell us where this man or number of men is to be found; whereas, surely this ought to have been of all things the most plainly and frequently urged in Scripture: it ought to have been as visible there as that God is one, or as that Jesus is Christ. Nay, indeed, methinks Scripture should have told us nothing else but where to find this infallible judge, and how to obey him. For all other precepts and rules of Scripture must certainly be some derogation to the power and authority of this infallible guide."—"*The Faith and Practice of a Church of England Man,*" by William Stanley, D. D., Dean of St. Asaph, Ch. v.

2. Because, in the nature of things, a translation is *only a translation,* and must be marked with the traces of human infirmity. Why, there are doubts and differences even in regard to *the original;*—unimportant, indeed, they are acknowledged to be, but still doubts and differences; and shall a *translation* have higher authority than its *original?* The thing is absurd.

3. Because, such a claim as that now put forth by the Romish Church was not thought of at the time it was published. This appears from its very Preface to the Reader, inserted in authorized editions. The language of that Preface is, that " *it is difficult to affirm*" *that this very edition,* revised and re-revised as it was, " *was absolutely perfect in all its parts, on account of human infirmity,*" * and further speaks of " *various readings,*"† which the apostolic

---

* "Accipe igitur Christiane Lector, eodem Clemente Summo Pontifice annuente, ex Vaticana Typographia veterem ac vulgatam Sacræ Scripturæ editionem, *quanta fieri potuit diligentia* castigatam; quam quidem sicut *omnibus numeris absolutam, pro humana imbecillitate affirmare difficile est,* ita ceteris omnibus, quæ ad hanc usque diem prodierunt, emendatiorem purioremque esse, minime dubitandum."—*Præf. ad Lectorem;* Biblia Sacra, *Vulgatæ editionis,* Lugduni, A. D. 1675.

† " Sed sicut Apostolica Sedes industriam eorum non damnat, qui concordantias locorum, *varias lectiones,* præfationes Sancti Hieronymi, et alia id genus in aliis editionibus inseruerunt; ita quoque non prohibet, quin alio genere characteris in hac ipsa Vaticana editione ejusmodi adjumenta, pro studiosorum, commoditate, atque utilitate in posterum adjiciantur; ita tamen, ut lectiones variæ ad marginem ipsius textus minime annotentur."—Ib.

chair at Rome did not forbid. Now these are things which are utterly discordant with the claims put forth in modern days. Even Cardinal Bellarmine, that prince of Jesuits, a chosen champion of the Romish Church, says,—we may have recourse unto the originals; "*First,* if through error of the Scribe, there be any place falsely written. *Secondly,* if the Latin copies do so far differ, the one from the other, that it is not known which is the true Vulgate reading. *Thirdly,* when, in the Latin, words or sentences are doubtful. *Fourthly* and lastly, for the finding out of the true and lively signification and propriety of either words or phrases in the Hebrew tongue."*

4. Because the Church of Rome, in making such a claim, stultifies herself.

At the time that the Council of Trent† stamped

---

* "Primo, quando in nostris Codicibus videtur esse error librariorum. Secundo, quando Latini Codices variant, ut non possit certo statui quæ sit vera vulgata lectio. Tertio, quando verba aut sententia in Latino est anceps. Quarto et ultimo, licet recurrere ad fontes, ad energiam, et proprietatem vocabulorum intelligendam."—Bellarmine, *De verbo Dei,* lib. II., c. ii., p. 120. James's "*Corruptions,*" etc. Part III., p. 355. London, 1688.

† The Council of Trent, after many delays and evasions on the part of the Papal Court, met on the 13th of December, 1545. Nothing of importance was done at the first two sessions. At the third session, Feb. 4th, 1546, the Nicene Creed—curiously enough—was declared to be the firm and only foundation against which the gates of Hell should never prevail, although the subsequent proceedings went to establish new and discordant articles of faith, utterly inconsistent with that pure and primitive symbol. The Council, at their *fourth* session, which met in

the Latin Vulgate as "authentic," *there was no such book in existence* as that which is now held to be, in consequence of their decree, "the full and correct copy" of the Holy Scriptures. This decree bears date, April 8th, 1546; and the authentic Vulgate was published November, 1592! Hence it appears that the Council of Trent was endowed with the gift of *prophecy,* as well as infallibility,—a gift which exalts their decree to a higher pitch of authority than Protestants ever imagined.* Contrary to their

April, 1546, proceeded to define the Canonical Scriptures. "Among the Prelates assembled," writes Fra Paolo Sarpi, the Romish historian, "consisting of five Cardinals and forty-eight Bishops, there was no one distinguished for learning. Some were lawyers, able, perhaps, in their profession, but ignorant on subjects of religion. Very few were theologians, and fewer still of more than ordinary capacity. The greater part were gentlemen and courtiers of mere titular dignity, and Bishops of places so small, that they could not be said to represent the thousandth part of Christendom." It might be added that, with the exception of Cardinal Pole (from England) and a few others, they were all Italians, and mere creatures of the Pope. There was not a single prelate or divine present from Germany.—"*Hist. Coun. Trent.,*" London, 1640, p. 163.

* The Council of Trent by no means harmonized the Romish Church. Afterwards, different parties were greatly divided on the questions of Divine Grace,—the Authority of Councils compared with that of Popes, —and the Immaculate Conception of the Virgin. In these disputes they mutually branded each other with heresy. The disputes between the Jansenists (Jansenius was Bishop of Ypres) and Jesuits, about 1640 and thereafter, were particularly bitter. See Palmer's "*Ecclesiastical History,*" Chap. xxiv. The doctrines of the Jansenists were similar to those which were elaborated and systematized by the famous Genevan reformer, John Calvin. See Appendix.

3*

own rules, the child was baptized "*in matris utero*," before it had seen the light!*

In consequence of the multiplication of copies rendered necessary from time to time, and the carelessness of transcribers, who sometimes intermixed the two versions—the old Italic, and Jerome's or the Vulgate,—with each other, new errors were continually introduced into the Latin text. This was partially remedied by Alcuin, at the command of Charlemagne in the eighth century, and Lanfranc, Archbishop of Canterbury, in the eleventh. But their efforts were of no material or permanent advantage; and the beginning of the sixteenth century found the text of the Latin Vulgate in sad confusion.

"Robert Stephens was the first who attempted to remedy this confusion, by publishing his critical editions of the Vulgate in 1528, 1532, 1534, 1540, 1545 and 1546. These, particularly the last, having incurred the censures of the Doctors of the Sorbonne, John Hentenius, a divine of Louvain, was employed to prepare a new edition. This he accomplished in 1547, in folio, having availed himself of Stephens's previous labors with great advantage."† The edition published in 1540 was Stephens's principal edition, and surpassed in magnificence every other.

A revised edition of the Vulgate was published

* "*Apol. Catholicæ*, Part ii., lib. i., Ch. ix., p. 32.—Tho. Morton, London, 1606.

† Horne, Vol. ii., Part i., Chap. v., Sec. 1.

by Lucas Brugensis, with other divines of Louvain, in 1573. Pope Sixtus V., however, not being satisfied with that edition, commanded a new revision to be made with the utmost care. To this work we are told that he devoted much time and attention; and that he corrected himself, "with his own hands," the proofs of the edition, which was published at Rome in A. D. 1590. This edition, Pope Sixtus V. pronounced to be "*the authentic Vulgate*," and ordained that it *should be adopted* "as such throughout the world."

This fact is abundantly proved by the declaration of Sixtus V. himself, prefixed to that edition. "Of *our certain knowledge* and *fullness of Apostolical power* we do ordain and declare that the edition of the Vulgate Bible of both Old and New Testament, which was received by the Council of *Trent* for *authentic*, without any doubt or controversy, is to be reputed and taken to be THIS ONLY EDITION, which being as well as was possible reformed and printed in our Vatican, our will and pleasure is, *and we do so decree it*, to be read throughout the whole Christian world, in all churches, with this our determination, that *first*, it was allowed by a general and joint consent of the whole Catholic Church and Holy Fathers; *secondly*, by a decree made in the late general council holden at Trent, and now, *lastly*, by the Apostolical authority and power which God has given us, and therefore is to be received and accounted, for a *true, lawful, authentic* and *undoubted* copy, (to be cited, and no other,) in all public and private Disputations, Lectures, Sermons, and Expositions."*

In farther proof and confirmation of this, there is an inscription, in letters of gold, in the Pope's Vatican, in honor of Sixtus Quintus, that, "commanded the Holy Scriptures, to be most accurately printed (or published) according to the prescript form of the Council of Trent."†

"This inscription," as Angelus Roccha expoundeth it,—a Romanist himself—"is the fourth inscription in the Vatican; set there for an everlasting monument of that wonderful and truly Apostolical care which Sixtus Quintus took in the printing

---

* " Ex certa nostra scienta, deque Apostolicæ potestatis plenitudine statuimus, ac declaramus, eam vulgatam sacræ, tam Veteris, quam Novi Testamenti paginæ Latinam Editionem, quæ pro authentica a Concilio Tridentino recepta est, *sine ulla dubitatione, aut controversia* censendam esse HANC IPSAM, quam nunc, prout optime fieri poterit, emendatam et in Vaticana Typographia impressam, in Universa Christiana Republica, atque in omnibus Christiani orbis Ecclesiis legendam evulgamus, decernentes eam prius quidem Universali Sanctæ Ecclesiæ, ac Sanctorum Patrum consensione, deinde vero Generalis Concilii Tridentini decreto, nunc etiam Apostolica nobis a Domino tradita auctoritate comprobatam, pro *vera, legitima, authentica,* et *indubitata,* in omnibus publicis privatisque disputationibus, lectionibus, prædicationibus, et explanationibus, recipiendam et tenendam esse."—SIXTUS QUINTUS, *in Bulla præfixa Bibliis suis.*—T. James, London, 1638, p. 352.

† " Sacram Paginam ex Concilii Tridentini præscripto quam emendatissiman divulgari mandavit."—"*Apology for 'Bellum Papale,' "* p. 320, in T. James's " *Treatise on the Corruptions,*" etc. London, 1688.

and correcting of the Vulgate Bibles according to the prescript form of the Council of Trent; whereunto he bent all his endeavors, and employed the strength of his wit and understanding; and, as I verily am persuaded, such, and so great were his pains, both by day and night, that they cannot be sufficiently recounted of any man. I was well acquainted with his labors in this kind; I have oftentimes observed them with a diligent eye, wondering with myself how he could endure it. For he read over every word of the Bible before the books were printed, although he was daily pressed with all the weighty business of the whole Christian world, and did effect many godly, heroical and pontifical acts. So then, he diligently perused and *corrected* every page of the Holy Bible; so as every book thereof might be read, according to a decree of the Council of Trent, with all its parts, as they have been usually read heretofore in the Catholic Church, and are at this present time contained in the old Vulgate Latin Bible. Neither was this sufficient. To show his worthy pains, when the Bibles, thus by his care and diligence amended, were newly printed, he *reviewed them sheet by sheet*, that he might be sure to have them well and *faithfully* printed (reviewed and corrected) before their coming abroad into the world."*

* "Quarta quæ sequitur inscriptio ingentem indicat curam, et vere Pontificiam, quam Sixtus Quintus toto suscepit conatu pro Bibliis

Nay, more than this, Sixtus V. himself declares: *" We ourselves, with our own hands,"* have *" corrected whatever errors had crept into the press."* *

Certainly, then, if ever infallibility dwelt at Rome, we might expect to find it here. If ever there was, under such auspices, a "full and correct" copy of the Holy Scriptures, this is the volume! But lo! no sooner had it been sent forth with the stamp of *authenticity* imprinted upon it, "by the decision of an infallible judge," than, Sixtus dying in August

Vulgatæ editionis emendandis, et imprimendis juxta Concilii Tridentini præscriptum. Qua in re præstanda tot ac tantos die noctuque perpessus est labores, quantis unquam verbis explicare nemo posset, ut mihi persuadeo, qui hujus generis labores re ipsa videns non semel tanquam oculatus testis obstupui. Universa enim Biblia, antequam prælo committerentur, ad verbum perlegit, etiamsi quotidie in omnes totius Christiani orbis curas, et gravissimas quidem totus incumberet, et in dies singulos, res sane pias, et heroicas, ac Pontifice dignas produceret. Sacrosanctam igitur paginam perlegit universam et emendavit; atque ita, ut omnes Sacri Codices, juxta ejusdem Concilii Decretum cum omnibus suis partibus legantur, prout in Ecclesia Catholica legi consueverunt, et in veteri Vulgata Latina Editione habentur. Nec eo contentus, universa item Biblia sic emendata, et *recenter impressa de integro perlegit,* ut *omnia fideliter recognita in lucem prodirent.* Quam rem Inscriptio, quæ infra legitur, apertis hisce verbis breviter patefacit."—Ang. Roccha, "*Biblioth. Vatic.*" p. 229. James, 320, 321.

* "Ea res quo magis incorrupte perficeretur, nostra nos ipsi manu correximus, si qua prælo vitia obrepserant."—SIXT. *in præfat.* James's *Treatise,* p. 319. The reader may now judge for himself of the gloss which Romish writers are wont to put upon this matter; that "Sixtus, being much offended with the number of faults which had found their way into his Bibles, proposed to review them, and have them more accurately printed, but was prevented by death." Thus writes J. Gretserus, a Jesuit. A similar assertion is made in the Preface to the Vulgate.

of the same year (1590), it was found to be so full
of errors that Clement VIII. caused it to be suppressed,* and published *another* "authentic" Vulgate in 1592! This is now the Latin Vulgate of
the Romish Church. The manifold contradictions
and discrepancies between these two authentic
editions† were pointed out by Thomas James,
chief keeper of the Bodleian Library, University of
Oxford, in his *"Bellum Papale"*‡ (London, 1600),
much, as he supposed, to the disparagement of the
infallibility which exalted them *both*, though dif-
fering from each other, to be the "authentic"
standards of God's holy Word. Mr. James, however, manifestly overlooked the self-evident truth
that *infallibility* was *progressive*, or he would not
have treated the subject so lightly. Infallibility in
1590 was not *so infallible* as infallibility in 1592!

---

* Mr Moran admits that the Sixtine Vulgate "was suppressed" by
reason of errors, all of which were not typographical. It seems strange
indeed that even typographical errors could occur under the eyes of an
infallible proof-reader. "Its duration," he says, "was short." Long
enough, however, for infallibility to nod. Mr. Moran's further assertion,
that "Sixtus V. himself *would have corrected* the errors which occurred
had he not been prevented by death," may be placed by the side of the
Pope's own declaration above, that he "*had corrected*" them ;—"nostra
nos ipsi manu *correximus.*"

† Clement VIII. corrected the Vulgate Bible in above two thousand
places, according to the Hebrew and Greek, when the contrary reading was established by Sixtus V.—"*Corruptions,*" etc. by James.
Part III., p. 328.

‡ A number of these discrepancies are given by Horne, in his "*Introduction.*"—Vol. II., Part I., Chap. v., Sec. 1.

The degree of its progression since, it would be hard to measure.   Assuredly, the same authority that could annul and reverse the decision of *one* infallible judge, might do so in regard to *any other.*   If it so please such authority, the very Latin Vulgate itself, now absolutely perfect and full and correct, may give place to one still more absolutely perfect and full and correct; and I ask, with all confidence as to his ability, why may not Pius IX. cause *another* revision to be made, and pronounce with equal infallibility the text thus revised to be "authentic;" even though it should differ as much from the Vulgate of Clement VIII. as that of Clement VIII. did from the authentic Vulgate of Sixtus V.?

So much as to the claims put forth on behalf of the Latin Vulgate as "a full and correct copy of the Holy Bible,"* on the ground of "the decision of an infallible judge in which we may confidently abide."

Very little need be added in reference to the *Douay translation.*   It has, of course, all the blemishes

---

* Even Mariana the Jesuit admits that there was abundance of errors in the Vulgate.   "Tridentini decreti verbis *vulgatæ editionis vitia* non probantur, quæ *multa esse* ex Codicum varietate colligebamus, librariorum certe incuria."   Jo. Mariana, *pro Edit. Vulg.,* Ch. xxi., p. 99.—T. James, p. 355.   Nay, more than this,—We affirm, he says, that the Hebrew and Greek were by no means rejected by the Tridentine Fathers, the Latin indeed to be approved, not so, however, that they deny that certain places *can be rendered more plainly,* or even *with greater propriety.*   "Contendimus Hebraica Græcaque haudquaquam a Tridentinis Patribus rejecta esse, Latina quidem probari, neque ita tamen, ut loca quædam apertius, aut etiam magis proprie verti posse negent."—Ib.

and defects of its original, the Vulgate, which, upon the authority of the learned writer above (T. James), contains in a single book of Proverbs no fewer than eighteen sentences that have crept into the text of St. Jerome through ignorance or stealth ;—sentences which are not found either in the Hebrew, or in regard to some of them, the Greek of the Septuagint, or the Latin of St. Jerome, according as it is set forth in the King's Bibles by Arias Montanus.* The following, as a single instance, is found neither in the Hebrew nor the Greek (Vatican text), although it is contained both in the Vulgate and the Douay translation. Proverbs, Chapter x. verse 4: "He that trusteth to lies feedeth the winds, and the same runneth after birds that fly away." Of course, it is not in King James's version.

Who is it, then, I ask, that "*adds*" to "the words of the Prophecy of this Book?" The translators of King James's version, or the authors of the Vulgate

---

* This version was originally made by Pagnini, a celebrated Dominican Friar, in the early part of the sixteenth century. He was distinguished for his acquaintance with the Oriental languages, and spent twenty-five years, with the approbation of Pope Leo X., in translating the Scriptures. His translation was afterwards revised by Arias Montanus, a Spanish Benedictine Monk, one of the Council of Trent, who was afterwards employed, in consequence of his great learning, in editing the Royal or Antwerp Polyglott Bible. This version renders the *Hebrew* and *Greek* words, translated *repent* in King James's version, by *pœnitet*, *pœniteo*, meaning precisely the same thing.—See "*The Confessional*," by Bishop Hopkins, Chap. iv.

and Douay Bible,—the English or the Romish Church?

But the Douay Bible *departs even from the Latin Vulgate,* where that version is generally correct, and so multiplies its errors. The Vulgate translates for instance, μετάνοια and μετανοεῖτε, by *pœnitentia* and *agite pœnitentiam,* the natural signification of which is, *penitence, repentance,* and *exercise repentance,* as any one may see by looking into a Latin dictionary. But the Douay has *penance* and *do penance,** except where its translators have been obliged to translate correctly to avoid a manifest absurdity, as in Hebrews xii. 17: "He found no

---

* "Properly considered, penance corresponds to what the Church of Rome inculcates under the term of satisfaction. 'According to the most ancient practice of the Church,' saith the Catechism of Trent, ' when penitents are absolved from their sins, *some penance* is *imposed*, the performance of which is commonly called *satisfaction*. Any sort of punishment endured for sin, although not imposed by the priest, but spontaneously undertaken by the sinner, is also called by the same name. It belongs not, however, to penance, considered as a sacrament ; the satisfaction which constitutes part of the sacrament, is *that* which is *imposed by the priest*.' From this it is easy to divine the motive which induced the translators of the Douay Bible to use their favorite phrase, 'do penance,' instead of the true meaning of the Greek, μετανοεῖτε, 'repent,' or, according to the Latin Vulgate, 'exercise repentance ;' for the readers of that version can form no other idea of ' doing penance ' except the performing of the penance directed by the priest, or at furthest, the voluntary imposition of some painful and laborious work, undertaken as a ' punishment ' and ' satisfaction ' for their sins ; and thus the Word of God is made to command, in appearance, one of the most dangerous corruptions of their system."— " *History of the Confessional*," by Bishop J. H. Hopkins, p. 58.

place of repentance." It would certainly have been very unkind and *unfilial-like*, in Esau, to have endeavored to make his old father *do penance!* and therefore, they render the word correctly—*repentance*—although the same word, both in Latin and Greek, in the same Epistle, Hebrews vi. 1, is translated "penance." The Douay gives the true meaning of the word in Hebrew xii. 17, in a note: "He found no way to bring his father to repent or *change his mind,*" *i. e.* in reference to the blessing. Beside, the Latin dictionaries give for *penance* not *pœnitentia,* but 1. *pœna,* 2. *supplicium,* 3. *culpœ expiatio;* and for *to do penance,* not *agere pœnitentiam,* but *culpam pœna luere.* In Luke xiii. 3, where the Vulgate has "nisi pœnitentiam habueritis" (unless ye *have* repentance, or penitence,) the Douay renders it "unless you shall *do* penance." Here the Latin is not susceptible at all of the very convenient sense which is put upon "*agere* pœnitentiam," and yet the Vulgate and the Douay are *both "correct"* upon "the decision of an infallible judge!"

Another and more striking departure from the meaning of the original is found in Ezekiel xviii. 21, where King James's version reads: "If the wicked *will turn* from all his sins that he hath committed," the Hebrew is יָשׁוּב, *to turn away.* The Septuagint*

---

* The Vatican text of the Septuagint, to which reference is made, was sanctioned by the same Sixtus V., who published the Vulgate in

renders it in Greek, ἀποστρέψη (turn away from).
Here Pagnini and Montanus, their own competent
and faithful interpreters, translated correctly into
Latin, " Cum *aversus fuerit* ab omnibus peccatis
suis "* (when he shall *turn away* from all his sins).
But the Vulgate has it, " Si autem *egerit pœnitentiam* " (if he will exercise repentance), and the
Douay departs more widely from the original,
translating it, " If the wicked *do penance* for all his
sins." And yet the authors, both of the Vulgate
and Douay Bible, were compelled to translate this
same word correctly thrice in this same chapter.
In the 24th, 26th, 27th verses, the Vulgate renders
it by *averterit*, and the Douay "if the just man *turn
himself away* from his justice," and "when the wicked
turneth himself away from his wickedness." The
same words precisely, both in the Hebrew and Septuagint, which at Ezekiel xviii. 30, are translated in
the Douay Bible, " Be converted and *do penance*
(for all your iniquities)," are translated in Ezekiel

1590. It was published in 1587, after the labor of eight years ; and
established by his decree, to be received and held by all ; and prohibition
was made, that no one should dare *change any thing* in this edition,
either by adding thereto, or taking therefrom. " Post octennii circiter
laborem prodiit opus an. 1587, Sixto V. dicatum, illiusque præmunitum
diplomati, in quo sancitur ut ab omnibus recipiatur et retineatur, et
prohibetur ne quis de hac editione audeat in posterum, vel addendo,
vel demendo, quicquam immutare."—"*Preface to the Septuagint*," Glas-
guæ, 1831.

* See Bishop Hopkins's interesting and instructive work, " *History
of the Confessional*," Chap. iv.

xiv. 6 (in the same Bible), "Be converted and *depart from* (your idols)."*

These instances are given as but specimens of what might be adduced, to show the wide departure of the Douay Bible from the original language in which the Scriptures were written. More might readily be pointed out;† but these are quite sufficient for my purpose. A *single flaw* is manifestly *fatal* to the character of any book which claims to be faultlessly correct on "the decision of an infallible judge." That the Latin Vulgate has not such absolute perfection—much less the Douay Bible—has been abundantly demonstrated. And it is equally plain that the Douay especially mistranslates and perverts the meaning of the original Scriptures, to uphold the errors of a system of religion which took its fixed shape and form at the Council of Trent, in the sixteenth century.

We deny not, indeed, that our own version may have its defects, such as are inseparable from human infirmity. Nor is it necessary that it should be otherwise. Our Saviour and his Apostles quoted from the Greek Septuagint as well as from the Hebrew, although they differ in many particulars from each other; and thus established the principle

---

* In the 30th verse, where King James's version reads "repent and turn yourselves," and the Douay "be converted and do penance,"— the original is literally, "Turn ye and cause to be turned."

† See Appendix.

4*

that literal exactness was not necessary to the general and doctrinal integrity of the Sacred Canon.* While, therefore, we claim not presumptuously for our version of the Holy Scriptures absolute perfection, so we know that it is a faithful translation of the original, and amply sufficient to answer all the ends for which Divine Revelation was given.

II. But we have yet to speak of the *true number* of the CANONICAL BOOKS of the Holy Scriptures.†

---

* "It is not necessary to the perfection of this instrument that it should be guarded by a perpetual miracle from the chances of literal errors. The general and doctrinal integrity of the sacred canon being preserved from corruption, there exists no obvious or necessary cause that the text should be preserved immaculate. How fully impressed with this conviction the inspired writers were, must be directly apparent from the use which they have made of the Septuagint, which was ever considered a free translation. Those who are best qualified to inform us on the subject have expressly declared, that the Apostles have quoted from that version Yet, while they are no where observed to follow it where it misrepresents the sense, they are frequently observed to quote it where it merely deserts the letter. While the circumstance of their writing in Greek clearly demonstrates the prevalence of that language among those early converts, it is observable they made no provision that the primitive church should possess a better translation of the Old Testament than that of the Septuagint. It must be therefore inferred from their practice, that they considered the literal errors of that translation a matter of minor importance."—"*An Enquiry into the Integrity of the Greek Vulgate or Received Text of the New Testament,*" by Rev. Frederick Nolan, p. 390. London, 1815. See also Horne, Vol. II., Part I.,·Chap. ix., Sec. 2; Marsh's Michaelis, Vol. I., p. 215; and Owen on the "*Modes of Quotation,*" p. 4.

† For a full and careful discussion of this subject, the reader is referred to the article CANON, in Smith's "*Dictionary of the Bible,*" by the Rev. B. F. Westcott. See also the same author's elaborate and exhaustive "*History of the Canon of the New Testament,*" pp. 594.

Our difference with the Church of Rome on that subject can be settled in very few words. Passing by the important and decisive considerations, that none of what are called the Apocryphal books are extant in Hebrew; that they were not accounted canonical by the Jews, or mentioned as such by either Philo or Josephus;* that they were not recognized or quoted by our Saviour and his Apostles; that they were certainly not regarded by "the Church," as in the Canon for the first four centuries,†

* "We have not myriads of books discordant and contradicting each other, but only twenty-two, which comprehend the history of all former ages, and are justly regarded as Divine. Of them, five belong to Moses, containing his laws and the traditions of the origin of mankind till his death. The interval of time from the death of Moses till the reign of Artaxerxes, King of Persia, who reigned after Xerxes, the Prophets who were after Moses wrote down what was done in their times in thirteen books. The remaining four contain hymns to God and precepts for the conduct of human life."—Josephus *contra Apion.*

† The provincial Council of Carthage (A. D. 397), strongly influenced by the prejudices of St. Augustine, who knew nothing of Hebrew, gives a list of Canonical Books similar to that of the Council of Trent. By Canonical, however, the Carthaginian Council, as Rev. Mr. Lowell very conclusively shows, "meant no such thing as we mean by it." (Lowell's "*Five Letters.*") It enumerates *five* books of Solomon in the list; that is, besides Proverbs and Ecclesiastes and the Song of Songs, which are in the Hebrew Canon, it pronounced to be his, not only what is called in the Septuagint the Wisdom of Solomon, but also the Book of Jesus the Son of Sirach, which was written eight hundred years after his (Solomon's) death ! This is the Canon, remarks Dr. Jarvis ("*Reply to Milner's End of Controversy,*" p. 51), "which, on the authority of a Council influenced by St. Augustine, and in direct opposition to St. Jerome, and to a translation executed under the patronage of Damasus the Bishop of Rome, in the fourth century,—the Council of Trent, in the sixteenth century, adopted and bound to be received under the penalty of a *curse !* "

and were established as inspired in the Western Church only in the fourth session of the Council of Trent; passing by all these considerations, which are themselves perfectly conclusive,—I come to THE VERY VULGATE ITSELF, the "full and correct," the uncorrupt, unmutilated record of God's will, as they tell us, and what do we find there?*

St. Jerome, the translator of the Latin Vulgate,† flourished in the latter part of the fourth century. He is justly regarded, both by Protestants and by Romanists, as the greatest and probably the most learned of the Latin fathers. "Not undeservedly does the Catholic Church extol St. Jerome, that greatest of divines, and stirred up of God to interpret the Sacred Scriptures, that it may *not be difficult to condemn the judgment of all those who either do not*

---

* It seems almost incredible that St. Jerome's Prefaces should have been bound up in the same volume with the Latin Vulgate; yet, nevertheless, so it is. The Providence of God has so ordered it, that as far as the Vulgate is concerned, the antidote accompanies the poison. But infallibility had grown wiser when the Douay Bible was published. St. Jerome must speak in an *unknown tongue.*

† The *Itala* or *old Italic*, to which reference is made on a preceding page (17), was a remarkably correct Latin translation of the *whole Scriptures*, made from the Greek in the Old Testament as well as in the New, probably in the second century. This translation, in consequence of numerous errors that had crept into the text, was, at the request of Pope Damasus, revised by St. Jerome (384). Of that revision the Book of Job and the Psalms only have been preserved. Before he finished the revision of this, however, St. Jerome had commenced a new translation from the original Hebrew of the Old Testament into the Latin; and this, with the translation which he made from the Greek of the New Testament, forms the basis of the present Latin Vulgate.

acquiesce in the studious labors of so eminent a doctor, or trust that they can do better or even equal to him."[*]

Ever since the seventh century,[†] the version which St. Jerome made[‡] has been exclusively adopted by the Roman Catholic Church, under the name of the Vulgate. A decree of the Council of Trent pronounced it *authentic,* and commanded that it alone should be used whenever the Bible is publicly read. Hence this translation has taken the place of the original; and when translations are made into other languages in the Roman Catholic Church, they are made, as in the Douay Bible, from the Latin Vulgate, in place of the languages (Hebrew and Greek) in which the Bible was originally written. It is remarkable that the Decree of the Council of Trent, passed 1546, and confirmed by Pius IV. 1564, which enumerates the several books contained in the Canonical Scriptures, does not include either the Prayer of Manasses or the Third and Fourth[§] Books of Esdras. These, however, are appended to the Latin

---

[*] Quare non immerito Catholica Ecclesia Sanctum Hieronymum Doctorem maximum, atque ad Scripturas sacras interpretandas divinitus excitatum ita celebrat, ut jam difficile non sit illorum omnium damnare judicium, qui vel tam eximii Doctoris lucubrationibus non acquiescunt, vel etiam meliora, aut certe paria, præstare se posse confidunt."—*"Præfatio ad Lectorem,* BIBLIA SACRA, *Vulgatæ Editionis."*

[†] Horne, "*Ancient Versions,*" Part I., Chap. v., Sec. 1.

[‡] With the exception of the Psalms. The old Italic Psalter, as corrected by St. Jerome, has been retained.—Horne.

[§] First and Second Esdras in the Apocrypha of King James's Bible.

Vulgate, "lest they should be lost;" but they are omitted altogether in the English Douay version. All the other books, however, designated as the Apocrypha in King James's Bible, are stamped by that Decree of the Council of Trent as "sacred and canonical;" and a solemn "*anathema*" rests upon the head of "any one that does not so hold them."*

"FROM THIS DECREE (in 1546) *it follows,*" I quote the language of the Preface to the Douay Bible itself, "*that all these books are of* DIVINE *and* INFALLIBLE *authority;* those, concerning which *some doubts were formerly entertained,* such as Judith, etc., as well as those which *have always* been venerated."

Now, *what does the learned* ST. JEROME *say in regard to these points?* that "maximus Doctor;" the translator of the very Vulgate itself; a man from whom no one may differ, or think he can surpass or equal, without condemning himself! *What does* ST. JEROME *say* IN THE VULGATE ITSELF?

First, he asserts that, as there were *twenty-two letters in the Hebrew alphabet,* so there were *twenty-*

---

* Rome has "anathematized not only the Anglican and all other Reformed Churches, but as well the ancient Churches of the East, who with us reject the Apocrypha and adhere to the Scriptures which were sanctioned by the Lord. We might speak more strongly of the danger of 'cursing whom God hath not cursed;' but we may rest satisfied with the assurance that 'the curse causeless shall not come.'"—Bp. Browne's "*Exposition of the Thirty-nine Articles,*" p. 158.

*two books in the Old Testament Scriptures.** He
then declares *what those twenty-two books are; enu-
merating precisely those books which are found in
King James's Bible* and *none others.* The First and
Second Books of Samuel, Kings and Chronicles
(or Paralipomenon) are not divided, and Ezra and
Nehemiah (First and Second Esdras) are counted
as one, as also the twelve minor Prophets. It is to
be observed, that he includes Ruth and Lamenta-
tions in this number, as forming a part of Judges
and Jeremiah respectively. But he goes on immediately to say that some enumerated them separately,
and that thus *the books of the old Law,* "priscæ legis
libros," were *twenty-four;* designating precisely
those which are contained as canonical in King
James's Bible.

But St. Jerome's language, as he proceeds, is, if
possible, still more striking. "This preface . . .
may answer," he writes, "for all the books which
we have translated from the Hebrew into Latin,
that we *may know* that *whatsoever is beyond these,
should be placed in the Apocrypha.*"* "Therefore,"

---

* "Quomodo igitur viginti duo elementa sunt, per quæ scribimus
Hebraice omne quod loquimur, et eorum initiis vox humana compre-
henditur; ita viginti duo volumina supputantur, quibus quasi literis et
exordiis, in Dei doctrina, tenera adhuc et lactens viri justi eruditur
infantia."—Hieronymi " *Prologus Galeatus* " (in the Latin Vulgate).

† " Hic prologus, Scripturarum quasi galeatum principium, omnibus
libris quos de Hebræo vertimus in Latinum, convenire potest; ut scire
aleamus, *quidquid extra hos est, inter Apocrypha esse ponendum.*

he adds, " Wisdom, which is commonly ascribed to Solomon, and the Book of Jesus the Son of Sirach (Ecclesiasticus), and Judith, and Tobias, and Pastor, *are not in the Canon.* The First Book of Maccabees I have found in Hebrew.* The Second is Greek, which may be proved from its very phraseology."

In speaking more particularly of " the Book of Jesus, Son of Sirach, and another counterfeit writing " (alius pseudepigraphus), which is called " the Wisdom of Solomon," he writes thus,—" as *the Church reads* indeed the books of Judith and Tobias, and Maccabees, but *does not receive them among the Canonical Scriptures;* so also these two books she may read for the edification of the people, but not to confirm the authority of any ecclesiastical doctrine."†

THE CHURCH does not receive them among the Canonical Scriptures! "*Ecclesia* non recipit." St. Jerome, then, does not give it as his "*private opinion,*" that these books ought not to be received in the

---

Igitur Sapientia, quæ vulgo Salomonis inscribitur, et Jesu filii Sirach liber, et Judith, et Tobias, et Pastor, *non sunt in Canone.* Machabæorum primum librum Hebraicum reperi. Secundas, Græcus est ; quod ex ipsa quoque phrasi probari potest."—Hieronymi " *Prologus Galeatus.*"

* Probably meaning the Syro-Chaldaic.—Dr. Jarvis, p. 46.

† " Sicut ergo Judith, et Tobiæ, et Machabæorum libros legit quidem ECCLESIA, sed *eos inter Canonicas Scripturas non recipit;* sic et hæc duo volumina legat ad ædificationem plebis, *non ad auctoritatem Ecclesiasticorum dogmatum confirmandam.*"—*Præfatio in Libros Salomonis.*

Canon, as Romanists would have us believe; but states *the fact* that THE CHURCH *did not receive them.* His *personal veracity* is, therefore, involved as a witness to a fact of which he could not be ignorant. Will Romish writers call this in question? Will they say that their "maximus doctor," the man who, their Vulgate asserts, was "divinely moved to interpret the Holy Scriptures," uttered a deliberate falsehood? Yet such is the alternative, if the Church in his day did receive the Apocryphal books, Judith, Wisdom, etc., as canonical. It is remarkable that the Church of England quotes this very observation of St. Jerome in her Sixth Article.

In his Preface to Jeremiah, we find the following: "We have omitted the Book of Baruch, his (Jeremiah's) secretary, which is *neither read* nor *received among the Hebrews:*" and further, in his Preface to Daniel, the Book of Daniel "among the Hebrews, has neither the history of Susanna, nor the Song of the Three Young Men, nor *the fables* (fabulas) of Bel and the Dragon,"* "which . . . we have added, the truth being stated before, and destroying their authority."

It will be readily seen, from the above extracts taken from the Vulgate itself, that St. Jerome's convictions about the Canonical Books of Holy

---

* "Qui apud Hebræos nec Susannæ habet historiam, nec hymnum trium puerorum, nec Belis, draconisque *fabulas.*"—*Præfatio in Danielem.*

Scripture accord exactly with the teaching of the Church of England, as shown in her Book of Common Prayer,* and her authorized copy of the Holy Scriptures. She accounts those books to be canonical, which he, St. Jerome, living within four hundred years from the birth of Christ, the *very translator* of the *Vulgate himself,* in the professed estimate of the Romish Church, the greatest and most distinguished of doctors, unapproachable by all for his learning and judgment,—decides to be such ; and she calls those Apocryphal which were so denominated by *him.* This, however, she does, not so much in submission to his sole authority, as in deference to the general voice of the EARLY CHURCH, to which he gave such striking utterance.†
Surely nothing but "the decision of an infallible judge in which we can confidently abide," could ever authorize us to differ from sentiments thus held and thus expressed ! ‡

* Sixth Article of Religion.

† The Romish Church, as it now exists, with its present Canon of Holy Scripture, including the Apocrypha and its Creed of Pius IV., 1564, bound upon the consciences of its members,—both unknown to the Primitive Church—cannot date farther back than the Council of Trent in the sixteenth century. It has, therefore, no rightful claim to Catholicity. Its creed is new ; its canon of Scripture is also new ; and be it remembered, that " whatsoever is truly *new* is certainly *false,*" as regards Divine Truth.

‡ Gregory Nazianzen flourished about A. D. 370. St. Jerome celebrates his eloquence, and called him his master whom he had heard interpreting the Scriptures,—" Vir eloquentissimus, præceptor meus, quo Scripturas explauante didici."—Among his poems there is one

These extracts illustrate the nature and gradual progress and development of Romish *infallibility.* St. Jerome was infallible in his *translation* where his "private opinion" might readily mistake; but he is not infallible in *his arrangements of the books* of Holy Scripture, even though he gave utterance therein to the united voice of the whole Church for four hundred years. Nay, it was not till *after the lapse of fifteen and a half centuries* that "an infallible judge" even *professed* to give "a decision in which all might confidently abide." "FROM THIS

which contains a catalogue of the Books of the Old and New Testament. Dr. Lardner, in his "*Credibility of the Gospel History,*" (Vol. IX., p. 132, London, 1753), gives it as follows: "Meditate and discourse much on the Word of God. . . . *But as there are many falsely ascribed writings, tending to deceive,* accept, my friend, this certain number. There are twelve historical books of the most ancient Hebrew wisdom: the first Genesis, then Exodus, Leviticus, Numbers, Deuteronomie; the next Joshua, the Judges, Ruth the eighth, the ninth and tenth the Acts of the Kings, and then the Remains, and Esdras the last. Then the five books in verse, the first Job, next David, then the three books of Solomon, Ecclesiastes, the Song, and the Proverbs. The prophetic books are five. The twelve Prophets are one book: Hosea, Amos, Micah, Joel, Jonah, Obadiah, Nahum, Habakkuk, Zephaniah, Haggai, Zachariah, Malachi. All these make one book. The second is Isaiah, then Jeremiah, Ezekiel, and Daniel. Which make twenty-two books, according to the number of the Hebrew letters. The books of the New Testament are as follows: Matthew wrote for the Hebrews, Mark for the Italians, Luke for the Greeks, for all that great herald John, enlightened with the heavenly mysteries. Next the Acts of the Apostles; fourteen Epistles of Paul; seven Catholic Epistles, which are these: one of James, two of Peter, three of John, one of Jude, which is the seventh." Revelation is quoted twice in Gregory's remaining works.

Decree (at Trent) it follows," etc. (Douay Bible,)
and so the Church for near 1600 years had to grope
her way in darkness. Her children had nothing
more to depend upon than the *fidelity and faith* of
the *Primitive Church,* in the first four centuries;
which, of course, could not be compared for a mo-
ment with the undoubted *infallibility* of the *Council
of Trent,* with its five Cardinals and forty-eight
Bishops in the sixteenth century.* I know it is

* Rev. R. T. S. Lowell, Rector of Christ Church, Newark, N. J., in his
correspondence with Rev. Mr. Moran, thus sums up the historical
evidence for our Canon: " The Canon of the present Latin Vulgate
has been reduced to the Council of Trent as the first ' *authority*' that
it can boast: Pope Gregory the Great condemns it in plain words at
Rome.

" Our Canon has cut off no other books than those which were rejected by the Jews. The Council of Laodicea (between A.D. 320 and
370) gives the same Canon, and was received by the whole Church.
The Council of Laodicea enumerates exactly our Canon as regards the
Apocrypha, and forbids the reading of any books than those enumerated. The Council gave the list of books that might be read in churches,
and left out Revelation, exactly as the Church Catholic then and as
now reformed in England and this country, does to-day.

" St. Cyril, Bishop of Jerusalem, or Patriarch, gives us just the same
in A.D. 386. St. Athanasius, Patriarch of Alexandria, contemporary
with St. Cyril, gives the same. St. Jerome—called translator of the
Latin Vulgate—gives the same, in the fifth century. The Greek Church
always had the same. Pope Gregory the Great bears witness to it
in the seventh century, from his seat in Rome. Cardinal Cajetan, in
the sixteenth, not only proves that Rev. P. Moran's canon was not
established, in the very Papal Church, in his day, but says that that of
Jerome (ours) was the true Canon. St Jerome says: The Church
knows no Apocrypha.

" If, now, your correspondent choose to bring up here the Carthaginian Council—the only thing that even *seems* (and it is only seeming)

said in the Preface to First Maccabees, in the Douay
Bible, that the Church, *i. e.* the Romish Church,
declared those two books canonical in *two* General
Councils, viz: *Florence* as well as Trent.   But then
the Council of Florence was held as late as A. D.
1440; and there are some strange stories told about
that period, which might possibly detract from its
authority; such, for instance, as the rivalry of *two
Pontiffs* and *two Councils,—each* party invested with
infallibility, and each *anathematizing the other.**   I
prefer, therefore, under the circumstances of the
case, to give in my adhesion, so far as infallibility

like an authority for his late Canon—St. Augustine's (contemporary)
language explains the language of the Council: '*In canonicis, autem,
scripturis,*' etc., that among canonical (or *ruled*) scriptures (that might
be read in churches) those which are received by all Catholic Churches
should be PREFERRED *to those which some do not receive,* etc., in which
he makes three ranks of different authority.   Cardinal Cajetan again
says, in so many words, that 'Fathers and Councils both must be
reduced to St. Jerome's standard:' '*Ad Hieronymi limam,*' etc., and
then goes on to say that we must understand *both St. Augustine and
the Carthaginian Council* according to 'this distinction, viz., that these
books (Apocryphal, by our Canon), ARE NOT CANONICAL, that is, ruled
for confirming matters of faith.'   This is most ample evidence, and just
before the Trentine Council."

   * The Council of Florence against the Council of Basil; and Pope
Felix V., the rival and opponent of Pope Eugenius IV.   Infallibility
pitted against infallibility.   Even the faithful were staggered as to where
their allegiance was due.   "The greatest part of the Church submitted to the jurisdiction and adopted the cause of Eugenius; while Felix
was acknowledged as lawful Pontiff by a great number of academies,
and among others, by the famous University of Paris, as also in several
Kingdoms and Provinces."—Mosheim, Vol. II., Cent. xv., Part II., Sec.
xiii.

is concerned, to the Council of Trent; *i. e.* provided I have the right to exercise any private judgment in the matter at all. Certainly, however, we of the seventeenth and eighteenth and nineteenth centuries, have great reason to be thankful that *we* know so *much more* in regard to the Canonical Books of the Holy Scriptures than the *Early Church*, even although an *infallible* authority decides that we *cannot differ from the opinion of St. Jerome without condemning ourselves.* To confess the truth, one finds himself here in an awkward dilemma; the decision of an infallible judge pointing out *two* courses in *opposite* directions, *both* of which must be taken at *the same time.* St. Jerome was *right*, and St. Jerome was *wrong!* St. Jerome held as apocryphal, Wisdom, and the Book of Jesus, and of Baruch, etc.; and we *must not differ* from his judgment, according to an infallible decision; and yet if we presume to contemn those books *as apocryphal*, we are *anathema!* Verily, it seems as if the comfort of having "an infallible judge, in whose decision we can confidently abide," must here fail us! Ah, happy Jerome! that was not called upon to meet the difficulty himself,—that kept both his saintship and his learning! It is just possible that he might have found himself in the predicament of the Philosopher in after years, who, as the story goes, humbly submitted to the decision of this infallible tribunal in regard to the solar system; and yet,

when going from the august presence, exclaimed,
as he stamped upon the earth, "Nevertheless, it
moves still!"*

"I speak as to wise men; judge ye," then, my
brethren, "what I say."† Decide for yourselves, if
not with the wisdom of infallibility, which belongs
to Him alone, "in whom are hid all the treasures
of wisdom and knowledge;"‡ yet, with the common

---

* "Cardinal Wiseman recently delivered a lecture at Leeds, in which
he asserted that Galileo was *not* persecuted for his scientific discoveries,
or as an astronomer, but for attempting to bend Scripture, contrary to
orthodoxy, to suit a scientific theory which he could not demonstrate.
The *Leeds Intelligencer* shows, from Galileo's own writings, that so far
from attempting to wrest Scripture to suit a theory, he held that Scripture was given for teaching the way of salvation, and not for informing
us about those natural phenomena with which our senses and intellect
can cope. The very words of the judgment, delivered and recorded
against him by an assembly named by the Pope, plainly prove that it
was his *science* and not his *theology* that was condemned. The judgment was as follows: 'To maintain that the sun is placed immovably
in the centre of the world (*i. e.* the solar system), is an opinion absurd
in itself, false in philosophy and formally heretical, because it is expressly contrary to the Scriptures. To maintain that the earth is *not* placed
in the centre of the world, that it is *not* immovable, and that it has even
a daily motion of rotation, is also an absurd proposition, false in philosophy, and at least erroneous in point of faith.' Subsequently, when
in his seventieth year, Galileo was obliged to abjure his astronomical
theory in the following terms: 'I abjure, curse, and detest the error
and heresy of the motion of the earth.' After this he was condemned to
perpetual imprisonment, and enjoined to perform sundry spiritual
exercises and penances for his heresy. So that the compounding of an
incongruous mixture of science and theology was the work of the papal
doctors, and not of the unfortunate Galileo."—Rev. H. Caswall, in the
" *Register*."

† 1 Cor. x. 15.   ‡ Coloss. ii. 3.

sense and reason that God hath given you, and which in this case are amply sufficient. If "God hath spoken unto the fathers by the Prophets," and "in these last days unto us by His Son;" and if the things thus revealed have been "written for our learning;" I ask where shall we find the authentic record of such Divine Revelation, if not in that Bible which has been the guide of our youth, and the companion of our maturer years—that Bible which tells us in our own tongue, "its glowing glorious English," the wonderful works of God?

We believe, therefore, and are sure,*—with a conviction in which no element of moral certainty is wanting,—that our authorized English version *is a full and correct copy of the Revelation of God's most holy will,* even of those Scriptures which, "given by inspiration of God," "are able to make us wise unto salvation through faith which is in Christ Jesus."† We believe and are sure, that "the signs which Jesus did" were written even as we have them there, that we "might believe that Jesus is the Christ, the Son of God; and that believing, we might have life through his name."‡

---

* St. John vi. 69.   † 2 Tim. iii. 15.

‡ St. John xx. 31.

APPENDIX.

—— •••• ——

Page 5.

"*Ne laici habeant libros Scripturæ præter Psalterium, et divinum officium; et eos libros ne habeant in vulgari lingua.*

"Prohibemus etiam, ne libros veteris testamenti aut novi, laici permittantur habere: nisi forte psalterium, vel breviarium pro divinis officiis, aut horas beatæ Mariæ, aliquis ex devotione habere velit. Sed ne præmissos libros habeant in vulgari translatos, arctissime inhibemus."—Hardouin's "*Acta Conciliorum*," Tom. vii. Paris, 1714, Col. 178, Capitulum xiv. *Concilium Tolosanum,* anno 1229, " de inquirendis hæreticis, deque aliis ecclesiasticæ disciplinæ capitibus celebratum." This Council was held in November, under St. Angelus, Roman Cardinal Deacon and Apostolical Legate.

Page 13, Note †

Beside the Versions of the Old Testament mentioned in the preceding discourse, there were also *Chaldee Paraphrases,* generally called Targums. Of these, ten are now extant. The Targums of Onkelos and Jonathan Ben Uzziel are the most highly prized. It has been supposed by some that Onkelos was contemporary with our Saviour. None of the others date farther back than the third century, with perhaps the exception of that of Jonathan. There were also, beside the Septuagint, the Greek versions of Aquila and Theodotion, both of which were executed near the middle of the second century, and of Symmachus, about the close of that century, with some anonymous versions of later date. Origen, in the early part of the third century, undertook the laborious task of collating the Greek text then in use, with the Hebrew and other translations then in existence, and from the whole to produce a new recension or revisal.—(Horne's "*Ancient Versions.*")—Twenty-eight years were devoted to the preparation of this arduous work, which has proved the lasting monument of his learning and piety. It is called by various names among ancient writers, as *Tetrapla, Hexapla, Octapla, Enneapla.*

PAGE 21, NOTE *

The version of the Geneva Bible was made by *the Refugees* in Queen Mary's reign, and printed at Geneva in 1560. Hence it is called the *Geneva Bible.* Sometimes it was called " The Breeches Bible," from Genesis iii. 7, where Adam and Eve are said to have sewed fig-leaves together to make themselves *breeches.* Coverdale and possibly Knox are supposed to have been among the number of the translators. " This," as Bishop Short affirms ("*History,*" Ch. xii., Sec. 537), " was a better translation than any before it." It contained various readings and marginal annotations, and other matters calculated to throw light on the meaning of the sacred text; and on that account was much esteemed. Thirty editions, either as folio, quarto, or octavo, were printed within fifty-six years. The division into verses was first adopted in this Bible.

The Old Testament was divided into sections and verses, marked off by points, perhaps as early as the time of Ezra ; a method adopted for the sake of interpreting it from Hebrew into Chaldee. The division into chapters is of much later date, and was made by Hugo de Sancto Caro, or Cardinalis, who composed the first Concordance to the

Vulgate, 1240. Robert Stephens divided the New Testament, and his son Henry printed it so, 1551. The following list of English versions is taken from Mant's *Preface*, Fuller's *History*, Lewis's and Johnson's *Historical Account* (original edition, 1730, London).

DATE.

706—Adhelm, Saxon, *Psalms.*

721—Egbert, *Four Gospels.*

734—Bede, *St. John's Gospel.*

880—Alfred, Version of the *Psalms.*

995—*Pentateuch*, etc., Elfric or Elfred.

1340—Rolle (of Hampole), *Psalms*, etc.

1380—Wyckliffe's *Bible.*

1526—Tyndal's *New Testament.*

1535—Coverdale's *Bible.*

1537—Matthew's *Bible* (*i. e.* J. Rogers's).

1539—Great *Bible* (Cranmer's, Taverner's).

1560—Geneva *Bible.*

1568—Bishops' *Bible* (Archbishop Parker).

1582—Rheims *New Testament.*

1609—Douay *Bible.*

1611—AUTHORIZED VERSION (King James).

PAGE 28.

DU PIN, the celebrated Romish historian, in his "*Complete History of the Canon of Scripture*," agrees with Bellarmine (see p. 28), in the expression of his views in reference to the Council of Trent. He admits, "that the intention of the Council was, that among all the *Latin* versions, this alone should be made use of in public sermons, disputes and conferences. This authentic qualification," he farther concedes, "however, does *not imply an exact conformity in all respects to the original writings, such as have*

been dictated by the Holy Ghost, or an exemption from all errors
whatsoever. But this version deservedly claims this title as
being *morally consonant* to the original," etc. "This version,"
he adds, "is commanded to be used without the least dimin-
ution of the authority and authentic qualification of the
original, or of the Chapter, *Ut veterum*, etc., 9: which
ordains: *Ut veterum librorum Fides de Hebrais voluminibus*
examinanda est, ita novorum veritas Græci sermonis normam
desiderat."—"*Dissertation on the Ancient Versions*," by Rev.
Thomas Brett, London, 1760, in Bishop Watson's Collection,
London, 1791.

Very moderate claims these, when compared with those
which now assert that the Latin Vulgate is full, correct and
uncorrupt (not infected with mistakes or errors), upon the
decision of an infallible judge! Verily, infallibility *is* progressive! It increaseth ever "more and more." *A Priest*
may now "confidently" assert, what a *Cardinal* would have
shrunk from saying two hundred and fifty years ago.

PAGES 28, 29.

The following is the original of the decree in regard to the
Nicene Creed, referred to in Note †, p. 28,—passed at the
third session of the Council of Trent—taken from an edition
of its Canons and Decrees, published at Antwerp, A. D. 1694.
De Symbolo Fidei, p. 17: "Quare Symbolum fidei, quo
Sancta Romana Ecclesia utitur, tamquam principium illud,
in quo omnes, qui fidem Christi profitentur, necessario con-
veniunt, ac *fundamentum firmum et unicum, contra quod*
portæ inferi numquam prævalebunt, totidem verbis; quibus
in omnibus ecclesiis legitur, exprimendum esse censuit, quod
quidem ejusmodi, est:—Credo in unum Deum Patrem
omnipotentem," etc.

PAGE 41, NOTE †

The following are additional instances of the little regard paid to the Hebrew by the authors of the Douay Bible, and the great latitude of translation in which they indulged.

In 1 Kings (3 Kings, Douay) viii. 35, where our authorized translation renders correctly, הוֹדוּ, "*confess* thy name," and the Septuagint ἐξομολογήσονται τῷ ὀνόματι σου, the Douay renders it "*shall do penance* to thy name;" while the *very same Hebrew word* is rendered in the Douay, 2 Chronicles (Paralipomenon), vi. 26, *confess to* thy name. The Septuagint has it in the one case *confess*, and in the other, *praise* thy name.

In Jeremiah xxxi. 19—"After that I was turned, I repented" (King James), the Douay translates, "after thou didst convert me *I did penance ;*" though the very same Hebrew word in 1 Kings (English authorized 1 Sam.), xv. 11, is translated "*it repenteth me* that I have made Saul king;" the Hebrew is נִהַמְתִּי. Thus there are at least three Hebrew words, which are translated *doing penance* in the Douay Bible; neither of which have any such meaning, and all of which have been rendered differently by the very authors of the Douay translation. In this text (Jeremiah xxxi. 19) the Hebrew word for convert, שׁוּב, is one which the translators of that version have also in other places rendered *do penance.* Consistently, therefore, they ought to have rendered this "after *that I did penance—*I did penance !"

.

NOTICES OF THE FIRST EDITION.

CANON OF HOLY SCRIPTURE; or, "*Is the Protestant Bible,—King James's Version,—the Word of God?*" With remarks upon the Latin Vulgate and Douay Bible, having special reference to the existing points of controversy between Protestants and Romanists. By Rev. MATTHEW H. HENDERSON, D. D., Rector of Emmanuel Church, Athens, Georgia, and formerly Rector of Trinity Church, Newark, New Jersey.

From Rev. SAMUEL H. TURNER, D. D., Professor of Biblical Literature in the General Theological Seminary, New York (1853).—"A MOST ABLE AND INTERESTING DISCOURSE."

From the Hon. THEODORE FRELINGHUYSEN, LL.D., President of Rutger's College, New Brunswick, New Jersey. May 4, 1853.—"Please accept my thanks for your kind remembrance in your excellent sermon on '*The Canon of Holy Scripture,*' A TIMELY AND CONCLUSIVE ARGUMENT."

From the Right Rev. J. H. HOPKINS, D. D., *Bishop of Vermont*, May 12, 1853.—"I am much obliged to your kindness for the copy of your excellent discourse, with its copious notes, upon 'THE CANON OF HOLY SCRIPTURE,' which I have read with much pleasure, none the less, from the evidence which it afforded that you had made some references to my own last work, 'The History of the Confessional.'"

From *The Newark Daily Advertiser.*—"For its *mild yet forcible logic*, its *solid and important information*, condensed into a compact compass, it deserves and undoubtedly will receive a careful perusal."

From *The Newark Mercury.*—"A *most able defence* of the Protestant version of the Scriptures. The fine taste of the writer has embellished it with passages of more than ordinary force and beauty."

Extract from a letter of THOS. B. MURRAY, Secretary of the Society for Promoting Christian Knowledge, 67 Lincoln's Inn Fields, London, Dec. 24, 1853.—" *Rev. and Dear Sir:* I have the honor to inform you that I duly brought under the notice of the Tract Committee of this Society your Treatise on the Canon of Holy Scripture. *His Grace the Archbishop of Canterbury had forwarded the work to the Committee for their inspection,* and it was accordingly referred for full consideration to a reverend and learned member of their body. That gentleman could not but see much that is excellent in the treatment of the very important and interesting subject you have taken in hand." . . .

The Archbishop of Canterbury (SUMNER) had become acquainted with the work through a personal friend (Rev. Mr. VALPEY), and he did the author the honor of requesting three copies, two for his chaplains, and one to be sent to the Society for Promoting Christian Knowledge. Subsequently the author received from him the following note:

" ADDINGTON LODGE, Nov. 17, 1853.

" *Dear Sir:* Your work on the Canon of Scripture has been offered to the Tract Committee, and by them referred to Dr. JELF, the Principal of King's College.

" He is at present out of town, but his answer may be soon expected. . . . . .

" I am, Dear Sir.
" Your faithful Servant,
" J. B. CANTUAR."

CPSIA information can be obtained at www.ICGtesting.com
Printed in the USA
LVOW131905040112

262376LV00012B/32/P